1. HEY, HEY, WHAT DO YOU SAY?
_____ IS HERE TO STAY!

OR: HEY, HEY, WHAT DO YOU SAY?
WE WANT A CONTRACT RIGHT AWAY!

HEY, HEY, WHAT DO YOU SAY?
_____ _____ALL THE WAY!

HEY, HEY, DON'T DELAY,
GIVE US A CONTRACT WITH EQUAL PAY!

HEY, HEY, WHAT SHOULD WE DO?
ORGANIZE OUR WHOLE DAMN CREW!

HEY, HEY, WHAT DO YOU KNOW?
_____IS MOVING MIGHTY SLOW!
(EX: THE BOARD, THE STATE, ETC.)

1

2. _____ _____IS UNFAIR,
    ALL WE WANT IS OUR FAIR SHARE!

3. WE'RE FIRED UP -
    WON'T TAKE NO MORE! (repeat)

4. WANNA KNOW WHAT ALL THE FUSS IS?
    WE ARE STANDING UP FOR JUSTICE!

5. ON STRIKE - SHUT IT DOWN,
    _____ IS A UNION TOWN!

   Or: ORGANIZE - DON'T FOOL AROUND
    _____ IS A UNION TOWN!

    UNION TOWN THRU AND THRU
    YOU FOR ME AND ME FOR YOU.

6. THEIR _____ PER CENT
    WON'T PAY THE RENT!

2

7. <u>CALL</u>   <u>RESPONSE</u>

    BOSS SAYS YES   WE SAY NO!
    BOSS SAYS HELL YES   WE SAY HELL NO!
    BOSS SAYS CUT BACK   WE SAY FIGHT BACK!
    BOSS SAYS GIVE BACK   WE SAY FIGHT BACK!
    BOSS SAYS TAKE AWAY WE SAY NO WAY!!!
    (a president's name, for example, can be substituted for "BOSS")

8. QUE QUEREMOS? JUSTICIA!
    CUANDO? AHORA!

9. WHAT DO WE WANT?   <u>JUSTICE</u>
     (or PEACE, PENSION, HOUSING, etc....)
    WHEN DO WE WANT IT?   <u>NOW</u>!

10. PUT ON THE HEAT, OUT IN THE STREET
    PEOPLE'S POWER CAN NEVER BE BEAT!!!

11. **AQUI ESTAMOS**
    Y NO VAMOS
    (Here we stand
    and we're not budging)

3

12. CALL	RESPONSE
NO CÓNTRACT	NO WORK!
NO CÓNTRACT	NO WORK!
NO DAMN CONTRACT	NO DAMN WORK!
NO DAMN CONTRACT	NO DAMN WORK!

13. WE'RE COLD, WE'RE WET
  CANCEL THE DEBT.

14. THERE'S ONE THING THAT'S
      CLEAR TO ME,
  THE PEOPLE HERE HAVE UNITY!

15. HEY, HÉY ---- HO, HÓ ----
  POVERTY WAGES HAVE GOT TO GO.

  Or: WHERE DID ALL THE MONEY GO?
      UNION POWER ON THE GO.
      UNION BUSTING'S GOT TO GO!
      _____ AND _____ HAVE GOT TO GO!

16. EL PUEBLO UNIDO JAMAS SERA VENCIDO!
  THE PEOPLE UNITED
  WILL NEVER BE DEFEATED!

4

17. ONE- <u>WE</u> ARE THE PEOPLE
TWO-A LITTLE BIT LOUDER
THREE-WE WANT_____
FOUR- NO STOPPIN' US 'TILL WE"VE
WON- WE ARE THE PEOPLE
TWO-A LITTLE BIT.....etc.

18. THIS IS WHAT DEMOCRACY LOOKS LIKE...
THIS IS WHAT DEMOCRACY LOOKS LIKE...

19. FEE FI FO FUM
LOOK OUT_____HERE WE COME

5

20. I DON'T KNOW BUT I'VE BEEN TOLD,
    BOSS'S POCKETS ARE LINED WITH GOLD!
    LIES AND TRICKS WILL NOT DIVIDE,
    WORKERS STANDING SIDE BY SIDE.

21. ESCUCHA, ESCUCHA
    ESTAMOS EN LA LUCHA!!!
        (Translation: Listen, Listen,
                      We're all in the struggle)

22. WE'RE GONNA BEAT ----- BEAT -----
      BACK THE BOSS
    WE'RE GONNA BEAT BEAT BACK
    THE BOSS   (yeah!)   or

    WE'RE GONNA BEAT ----- BACK -----
       THE _____ATTACK
    WE'RE GONNA BEAT BACK THE
        ___ _____ATTACK!

23. HELL NO, WE WON'T GO
     WE WON'T GO FOR TEXACO.

6

artist unknown·

24. **WE'RE BAD ----- WE KNOW IT -----**
    WE'RE HERE ---- TO SHOW IT--------
    WHAT YOU SEE IS WHAT YOU GET
    AND YOU AIN'T SEEN NOTHING YET!

25. **CALL**   **RESPONSE**

    DIGNITY   **UNION YES!**
    JUSTICE   **UNION YES!**
    RESPECT   **UNION YES!**
    ORGANIZE   **UNION YES!** etc...

26. **_____IS A WARRIOR -HOO(2X)**
    EVERYWHERE YOU GO,
    YOU CAN HEAR THEM SAY
    _____IS A WARRIOR!-HOO(2X)

MUSICAL NOTATION IN THE BOOKLET IS BY MARTHA BANZHAF

7

27. SIGAW NG BAYAN – KAPAYAPAAN
(Cry of the People – PEACE) (in Tagalog)

28. <u>CALL</u>   <u>RESPONSE</u>

WE ARE THE _____   WE ARE THE _____
MIGHTY MIGHTY _____   MIGHTY MIGHTY ____
EVERYWHERE WE GO   EVERYWHERE WE GO
PEOPLE WANT TO KNOW   PEOPLE WANT TO KNOW
WHO WE ARE   WHO WE ARE
SO WE TELL THEM...   SO WE TELL THEM...
  (Union, People, etc.)   (go to beginning)

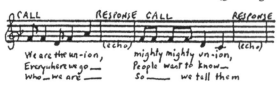

29. (Traditional Army marching tune)

        CALL: RESPONSE:

UNION POWER ON   NOW'S THE TIME
      THE RISE   TO ORGANIZE
NO MORE BOSSES'   "
      TRICKS AND LIES
GIVE OUR CHILDREN   "
      BETTER LIVES
TELL THE WOMEN   "
      TELL THE GUYS
ORGANIZE - ORGANIZE ... "

8

30. <u>CALL</u>   <u>RESPONSE</u>

   NO WORK   NO PEACE
   NO JUSTICE   NO PEACE
   NO HOUSING   NO PEACE
   NO HEALTH CARE NO PEACE

31. WHO'S GOT THE POWER?
   WE GOT THE POWER.
   WHAT KIND OF POWER?
   _____POWER!!!!

32. <u>CALL</u>   <u>RESPONSE</u>

   POWER - POWER - POWER- POWER BY THE HOUR
   UNION'S GOT THE POWER   "
   WORKING PEOPLE'S POWER   "
   POWER - POWER - POWER   "

33. WE'VE GOT _____ POWER, POWER, POWER
   IT'S THE GREATEST POWER OF THEM ALL.

34. TRUSTEES CEASE YOUR MYTHIC FABLE
    RETURN RIGHT NOW TO THE
       BARGAINING TABLE.

35. 1- 2 -3- 4   WE KNOW WHAT WE'RE OUT HERE FOR!
    or: NO ONE SHOULD BE WORKING POOR!
    or: WE WON'T TAKE IT ANYMORE!

    5 -6 -7- 8 SIT DOWN AND _____ NEGOTIATE!
    or: COME ON _____ PLAY IT STRAIGHT.
    or: WHERE'S OUR CONTRACT - WHY SO LATE?

36. WHO'S GOT THE MONEY?????????????????

37. GET UP - LEVANTATE!!
    STAND UP FOR YOUR RIGHTS.
    GET UP - LEVANTATE!!
    DON'T GIVE UP THE FIGHT.

38. SE VE, SE SIENTE
    LA UNION ESTA PRESENTE!!
         (Translation: See us! Feel us!
                    The union is here)

39. UN DANO PARA UNO
    ES UN DANO A TODO!!
         (Translation: An injury to one is
                    an injury to all.)

40. AW....TOOT! TOOT!
    GET UP OFF OF THAT LOOT !!!!

41. SERVE THE NEEDY
NOT THE GREEDY!!!

42. WE'RE OVERWORKED AND UNDERPAID
ARE YOU READY TO FIGHT? DAMN RIGHT!!!

43. MORE MONEY, MORE MONEY, MO
DO THE RIGHT THING, DO THE RIGHT THING
DO IT!!!

FACULTY WORKERS

44. WE'RE <u>WORKING FAMILIES</u> UNDER ATTACK
(HEALTHCARE WORKERS, etc.)
WHAT DO WE DO?
STAND UP! FIGHT BACK!

45. FIRE THE LIAR
IMPEACH___NOW!!

**46. WE CAN'T FIND OUR WAGES
IN THE YELLOW PAGES.**

47. UP WITH THE UNION   YEAH!!   YEAH!!
      DOWN WITH THE BOSSES   BOOM!!   BOOM!!
      THE DIRTY BOSS   "   "
      THE CHEAP BOSS   "   "
      THE LYING BOSS   "   "

**48. WE'RE OUT OF THE OFFICE
AND ONTO OUR FEET.
WE'RE OFF OF OUR _____
AND OUT IN THE STREET.**

49. HEY <u>BOSSES</u> CAN YOU HEAR IT?   (repeat)
      CAN YOU HEAR <u>OUR UNION</u> SPIRIT?   (repeat)
      GONNA ROCK YOU FROM BEHIND   (repeat)
      AND--BLOW---YOUR---MIND!!!

     (our mighty spirit may be substituted)

12

50. **CALL**   **RESPONSE**

CALL	RESPONSE
CUTS IN HEALTH CARE!	NO MORE!
UNDERSTAFFING!	NO MORE!
CUTTING CORNERS	NO MORE!
STAND UP FOR PATIENTS!	RIGHT NOW!
BETTER STAFFING!	RIGHT NOW!
BETTER FUNDING!	RIGHT NOW!

51. HEY_____, IT'S ABOUT TIME
WHAT YOU PAY US IS A CRIME
HEY_____, HEAR OUR CRY
WE NEED A PENSION, THAT'S NO LIE.

52. **CALL**   **RESPONSE**

CALL	RESPONSE
WE NEED STAFF	THEY JUST LAUGH
WE NEED SUPPLIES	THEY ROLL THEIR EYES
WE NEED MONEY	THEY THINK IT'S FUNNY
BUT IF WE FIGHT	THEY'LL DO WHAT'S RIGHT!!!

(handwritten: A CONTRACT ... tell us lies)

13

53. WHAT'S DISGUSTING?
    UNION BUSTING!!!

54. WHAT'S OUTRAGEOUS?
    SWEATSHOP WAGES!!!

55. JUST SAY NO TO _____'S LIES
    DEFEND OUR RIGHT TO ORGANIZE!
      Or: STOP THE THREATS, STOP THE LIES
          IT'S OUR RIGHT TO ORGANIZE!

56. WHAT DOES _____HAVE TO HIDE??
    SWEATSHOP PRODUCTS MADE INSIDE.

57. SWEATSHOP LABOR? NO WAY!!
    GET____AND MAKE THEM PAY.

14   DETAIL FROM A PAINTING BY OSCAR NUNEZ FROM

58. (Traditional army marching tune)

_____IS A UNION TOWN   (Repeat each line)
YOU CAN'T KEEP THE PEOPLE DOWN.

UNION TOWN THROUGH AND THROUGH
YOU FOR ME AND ME FOR YOU.

_____IS A UNION CITY
THE WAY YOU TREAT US IS A PITY.

UNION CITY IN AND OUT
WE WON'T REST UNTIL YOU'RE OUT.

59. BE FAIR----TO THOSE WHO CARE.

60. _____,_____DO WHAT'S RIGHT
PEACE & JUSTICE NOW! HO!!
UNION CONTRACT NOW! HO!!

Used by Permission

61. I SAID MY FEET ARE ACHIN',
MY SHOES' TOO TIGHT
MY HEART IS BREAKIN',
'CAUSE THINGS AIN'T RIGHT
LET ME HEAR IT NOW
_____(CONTRACT, HEALTHCARE)
ENOUGH IS ENOUGH!!!
WE MUST RISE UP!!!
DIDN'T EAT TODAY, GOT BILLS TO PAY
KISS THE BACK OF MA' B... (HUH)
KISS THE BACK OF MA' B... (HUH)
KISS THE BACK OF MA'
KISS THE BACK OF MA'
KISS THE BACK OF MA' B... (HUH)!!!

62. CALL :
  WHEN I SAY "UNION" YOU SAY "YES" (2x)

CALL:	UNION	
RESPONSE:	YES	}4X

CALL
  WHEN I SAY "ORGANIZE" YOU SAY "NOW" (2x)

CALL:	ORGANIZE	
RESPONSE:	NOW, etc....	}4X

  and...
    WHEN I SAY " HEALTH CARE".........
    YOU SAY "FOR ALL"......etc...

    WHEN I SAY "JUSTICE".............
    YOU SAY "FOR ALL"...... etc....

    WHEN I SAY "CUTBACK".........
    YOU SAY "NO WAY".....etc....

    WHEN I SAY " SI SE ".............
    YOU SAY "PUEDE"......etc

63. LISTEN_____HEAR OUR CRY
        WHEN WE"RE SCREWED WE MULTIPLY!!

        HEAR US THUNDER, HEAR US ROAR
        YOU CAN"T SCREW US ANYMORE!!
(This can be chanted to the traditional army tune)   17

64. WE'RE_____WORKERS ---FIGHTING BACK!
   WE'RE_____WORKERS ---FIGHTING BACK!
   (HOSPITAL, NURSING HOME, CAFETERIA...)

65. WE ARE UNION (Tune: We Will Rock You)

   (THUMP, THUMP   CLAP-----)
   (THUMP, THUMP   CLAP-----)
   (THUMP, THUMP   CLAP-----)
   (THUMP, THUMP   CLAP-----)

WE ARE, WE ARE UNION!
WE ARE, WE ARE UNION!

66. HYGIENISTS AND SCHOOL NURSES
   ALL NEED MONEY IN THEIR PURSES.

18

67. AQUI, ALLA
   EL PUEBLO VENCERA.
   (trans: Here, there. The people will win.)

68. <u>OLE</u>
 (Tune - Best known for the Toyota commercial)

   OLE (chanted 8X)
   _____'S HOT, HOT, HOT!!!

   (AND_____IS NOT, NOT, NOT!!!) or

   OLE (4x)
   PACK YOUR BAGS AND GO AWAY, etc. or
   _____IS HERE TO STAY.

69. _____RICH AND RUDE
WE DON'T LIKE YOUR ATTITUDE.

70. UNO, DOS TRES, CUATRO
QUE QUEREMOS UN CONTRATO.
(trans:1-2-3-4, We want a contract!)

71. _____SHAME ON YOU!!!

20

DIVIDED WE FALL!

72. WE AIN'T NOBODY'S WORKING SLAVE
WE DESERVE A LIVING WAGE.

73. _____ YOU'RE NO GOOD
SIGN A CONTRACT LIKE YOU SHOULD!!

74. <u>CALL</u>   <u>RESPONSE</u>

SE PUEDE ?   SI SE PUEDE!
CAN WE?   YES WE CAN! (Trans.)

SI SE PUEDE! SI SE PUEDE! SI SE PUEDE!
(Chant with clapping)

21

75. MONEY FOR HEALTH,   NOT FOR WAR
MONEY FOR LEVEES,   NOT FOR WAR
MONEY FOR FOOD,   NOT FOR WAR
MONEY FOR SCHOOLS,   NOT FOR WAR

76. WHOSE STREETS?   OUR STREETS!!

77. MAKIBAKA! HUWAG MATAKOT!
(Dare to struggle. Don't be afraid) in Tagalog

78. HO HO! HEY HEY!
IMMIGRANTS NEED RIGHTS TODAY!

79. SHAME SHAME SHAME
NOT IN OUR NAME!

80. MOVE OUT THE WAY_____.
MOVE OUT THE WAY!

81. BEEP BEEP!
_____'S CHEAP.

22

82. WHAT ARE OUR KID'S DYING FOR?
OUR GRIEF IS NOT A CALL FOR WAR.

83. AIN'T NO POWER LIKE THE POWER OF THE PEOPLE
AND THE POWER OF THE PEOPLE DON'T STOP
DON'T STOP!!
AIN'T NO POWER LIKE...etc.

(or CAUSE THE POWER OF THE PEOPLE IS ON FIRE!)

84. THE PEACE ROUND

Now, more than ever, we need this healing song.

PEACE, PEACE, PEACE, PEACE,
WARS HAVE BEEN AND WARS MUST CEASE
WE CAN LEARN TO LIVE TOGETHER
PEACE, PEACE, PEACE.

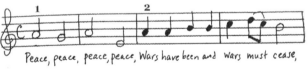

Peace, peace, peace, peace, Wars have been and Wars must cease,

We must learn to live to~ge~ther. Peace, peace, peace.

23

86. DE COLORES

This wonderful old Spanish song is ofen heard at immigration rights rallies, on the United Farm Workers picketline and at many celebrations. It's my favorite song!!

DE COLORES, DE COLORES SE VISTEN LOS CAMPOS
    EN LA PRIMAVERA
DE COLORES, DE COLORES SON LOS PAJARITOS
    QUE VIENEN DE AFUERA
DE COLORES, DE COLORES ES EL ARCO IRIS QUE
    VEMOS LUCIR.

    CHORUS (CORO)
        Y POR ESO LOS GRANDES AMORES DE MUCHOS
        COLORES ME GUSTAN A MI (2X)

CANTA EL GALLO, CANTA EL GALLO CON EL
    KIRI, KIRI, KIRI, KIRI, KIRI
LA GALLINA, LA GALLINA CON EL CARA, CARA,
    CARA, CARA, CARA
LOS POLLUELOS, LOS POLLUELOS CON EL PIO,
    PIO, PIO, PIO, PI

    CHORUS (CORO)......

Translation: See the colors, ah, the colors that cover
              the valleys and hills in the springtime
              See the colors, ah the colors that feather
              the birds flying in from far places.
              See the colors, ah the colors that arch
              over heaven in rainbows so bright

Chorus: How I love to enjoy all the colors, the reds,
            blues and yellows,
            So pleasing to me (2x)

24

De__ co-lo-res, de co-lo-res se
vis-ten los cam-pos en la pri-ma-ve-ra,__
De __ co-lo-res, de co-lo-res son los pa-ja-
ri-tos que vie-nen de a-fue-ra, __ De __ co-
lo-res, de co-lo-res es el ar-co i-ris que
ve-mos lu-cir y por e-so los gran-des a-
mo-res de mu-chos co-lo-res me gus-tan a mi
y por e-so los gran-des a-mo-res de mu-chos
co-lo-res me gus-tan a mi.

25

86. **UNION**   (Tune: AMEN)
   Chorus:
   UNION, UNION, UNION, UNION,
   UNION   (or FREEDOM etc...)
   Verses:
   1. UNION (EVERYBODY NOW)
      UNION (STAND TOGETHER)
      UNION, UNION, UNION.

   2. UNION (WE CAN MAKE IT)
      UNION (THEY CAN'T TAKE IT FROM US)
      UNION, UNION, UNION.

   3. UNION   (RAISE YOUR VOICES)
      UNION (SING FOR JUSTICE)
      UNION, UNION, UNION.

87. **UNION CONGA**
   (HERE Local 2 – San Francisco, Calif.)

         DO-THE-CON-GA
            DO THE UNION CONGA.
         SIGN-THE-CON-TRACT
            SIGN THE UNION CONTRACT.
         JOIN-THE PICK-ET
            JOIN THE UNION PICKET.
         DO-THE-RIGHT-THING
            UNION IS THE RIGHT THING!!!

26

88. YOU SCREWED US OVER

(Tune: Hey! Look Me Over) Words: Author unknown

YOU SCREWED US OVER
THAT'S WHY WE SAY
WE'RE GONNA WATCH YOU
EACH AND EVERY DAY. (or "come election day")
SO DON'T TURN YOUR BACKS BOYS
DON'T FEEL SECURE
WE'RE GONNA GET YOU IN THE END
OF THAT YOU CAN BE SURE
AND WE'LL BE BACK BY THE MILLIONS
YOU KNOW IT'S TRUE
HANG ON TO YOUR ASS, BOYS
WE'RE COMING AFTER YOU
HERE IS THE LESSON WE'VE LEARNED
THIS YEAR
ON THIS YOU CAN RELY

**WHEN WE'RE SCREWED
WE MULTIPLY!!!**

27

89. **WE SHALL NOT BE MOVED**

(Tune: Traditional)

Chorus:

WE SHALL NOT, WE SHALL NOT BE MOVED
WE SHALL NOT, WE SHALL NOT BE MOVED
JUST LIKE A TREE THAT'S STANDING BY
   THE WATER
WE SHALL NOT BE MOVED.

Verses:

1. THE UNION IS BEHIND US
         WE SHALL NOT BE MOVED (2X)
         JUST LIKE A TREE etc.

2. WE'RE BLACK, BROWN, WHITE TOGETHER...

3. WE'RE SINGING FOR OUR CHILDREN

4. WE'LL STAND AND WORK TOGETHER

5. WE'RE OLD AND YOUNG TOGETHER

BUT...

_____AND HIS CRONIES
         THEY SHALL BE REMOVED (2X)
   JUST LIKE A CAN OF GARBAGE
         IN THE ALLEY
         THEY SHALL BE REMOVED.

28

Chorus in Spanish:

1. NO., NO, NO NOS MOVERAN
   NO, NO, NO NOS MOVERAN
   COMO UN ARBOL FIRME JUNTO AL RIO
   NO NOS MOVERAN   or...

2. FUERTES, FUERTES, FUERTES SOMOS YA
   FUERTES, FUERTES, FUERTES SOMOS YA
   COMO UN ARBOL FIRME JUNTO AL RIO
   FUERTES SOMOS YA.

Spanish verses

1. UNIDOS VENCEREMOS....NO NOS MOVERAN
                or FUERTES SOMOS YA
2. UNIDOS EN LA LUCHA
3. UNIDOS EN LA HUELGA
4. LUCHAMOS POR LOS HIJOS   etc...

29

91. WHEN WE WIN A LIVING WAGE

(Tune: When the Saints Go Marching In)
(Words: Julie Mc Call
      Christine Haupert-Wemmer)

Chorus
WHEN WE WIN A LIVING WAGE
WHEN WE WIN A LIVING WAGE
OH, I WANT TO BE IN THAT NUMBER
WHEN WE WIN A LIVING WAGE.

Verses
AND WHEN THE BOSSES EARN THEIR PAY...

WHEN EVERY WORKER HAS A JOB...

WHEN HEALTHCARE'S FREE FOR YOU
  AND ME....

WHEN EQUAL WORK GETS EQUAL PAY...

Last Verse:
WHEN EVERY WORKER'S ORGANIZED
WHEN EVERY WORKER'S. ORGANIZED
WE WILL ALL BE THERE IN NUMBERS
WHEN EVERY WORKER'S ORGANIZED!!!

92. SHARE THE DOUGH

(Tune: "Let it Snow")
(New words: Julie McCall)

WHILE THE MINIMUM WAGE IS FRIGHTFUL
FOR THE WEALTHY LIFE'S DELIGHTFUL
TELL THOSE MILLIONAIRE CEO'S
SHARE THE DOUGH, SHARE THE DOUGH,
   SHARE THE DOUGH!

THE BATTLE AROUND US RAGES
AS WE FIGHT FOR LIVING WAGES
AND WE WANT TO GET WHAT WE'RE OWED
SHARE THE DOUGH, SHARE THE DOUGH,
   SHARE THE DOUGH!

Chorus
WE LEAVE FAMILIES HOME AT NIGHT
WORKING TWO JOBS IS THE NORM
AND WE KNOW THAT IT'S JUST NOT RIGHT
THIS SYSTEM NEEDS SOME REFORM.

THE ECONOMY'S GLOBALIZING
IN THE STREETS WE'RE ORGANIZING
AND WE'RE MAKING OUR MOVEMENT GROW
SHARE THE DOUGH, SHARE THE DOUGH,
   SHARE THE DOUGH!!!

93. __WE SHALL OVERCOME__
(Traditional)

1. WE SHALL OVERCOME
   WE SHALL OVERCOME
   WE SHALL OVERCOME   SOME DAY

Chorus

0-O-OH DEEP IN MY HEART
I DO BELIEVE
WE SHALL OVERCOME SOME DAY.

Verses:

2. WE SHALL LIVE IN PEACE (3x)
        SOMEDAY...etc.
3 TRUTH SHALL MAKE US FREE...
4 WHOLE WIDE WORLD AROUND...
5. WE'LL WALK HAND IN HAND...
        TODAY

Spanish:

UNIDOS VENCEREMOS
   (2X)
UNIDOS VENCEREMOS
   HOY
O-O-OH EN MI
   CORAZON
YO CREO
UNIDOS VENCER-
   EMOS

94. WE WISH YOU A MERRY CHRISTMAS

New words: Julie McCall

Chorus:
WE WISH YOU A HAPPY HOLIDAY (3X)
AND A JOYOUS NEW YEAR.

Verses:
WE THANK ONE AND ALL
FOR SUPPORT THAT YOU BRING
THROUGH THE HALLS OF OUR OFFICE
SOLIDARITY RINGS.

A CONTRACT TAKES TALK
AND TALKING TAKES TWO
WITHOUT GOOD-FAITH BARGAINING
THERE'S NO PEACE FOR YOU.

ON KWANZA OR CHRISTMAS
AND HANNUKAH, TOO.
A SEASON OF JUSTICE
IS OUR WISH FOR YOU.

Alternate Chorus:
(UNITE-Plastonics strike)
WE WISH YOU A MERRY CHRISTMAS
WE DON'T WANT TO STOP YOUR BUSINESS
BUT WE REALLY NEED A CONTRACT
AND WE NEED IT RIGHT NOW.

(**NOTE**: For more amazing holiday and other union songs
and creative strategies check out: www.laborheritage.org)

95. **LISTEN** (Tune: Frere Jacques)

LISTEN_____ (2X)
DO YOU HEAR?   (2X)
WE WANT _____ (2X)
IS THAT CLEAR?   (2X)

96. **THE UNION IS A LION**

1199- Sung on the Avery Heights Picket Line
Hartford, Ct.   Tune-Traditional

YOU'RE WRONG TO TROUBLE THE UNION
YOU'RE WRONG.
YOU'RE WRONG TO TROUBLE THE UNION
YOU'RE WRONG.
THE UNION IS A LION
THE LION WILL DEVOUR YOU.
YOU'RE WRONG TO TROUBLE THE UNION
YOU'RE WRONG.

(and: TROUBLE THE PEOPLE......THE WORKERS, etc)

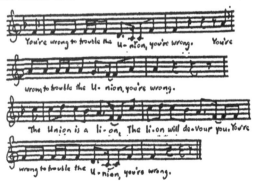

97. **THIS LITTLE LIGHT OF MINE**
(Traditional)

Chorus:
THIS LITTLE LIGHT OF MINE
  I'M GONNA LET IT SHINE
THIS LITTLE LIGHT OF MINE
  I'M GONNA LET IT SHINE
THIS LITTLE LIGHT OF MINE
  I'M GONNA LET IT SHINE
LET IT SHINE, LET IT SHINE, LET
  IT SHINE.

(or: WE'RE GONNA LET IT SHINE....)

Verses:
  1. UP AND DOWN OUR STREETS
      WE'RE GONNA LET IT....
  2. WE'VE GOT THE LIGHT OF FREEDOM
  3. ON THE PICKETLINE
  4. EVEN ON OUR JOB!!
  5. EVERYWHERE WE GO
  6. AIN'T NOBODY GONNA " WHOOF" IT OUT
      (hold up your index finger and "blow it out")

98. STUDY WAR NO MORE

Verse:
**I'M GONNA LAY DOWN MY SWORD AND SHIELD
DOWN BY THE RIVERSIDE (3X)
I'M GONNA LAY DOWN MY SWORD AND SHIELD
DOWN BY THE RIVERSIDE
STUDY WAR NO MORE.**

Chorus:
**I (OR WE) AIN'T A-GONNA STUDY WAR
NO MORE (6X)**

Additional verses:
**WE'RE GONNA JOIN HANDS AROUND
THE WORLD...**

**WE'RE GONNA SING OUT
UNTIL WE'RE HEARD...**

**WE'RE GONNA VOTE YOU OUT
OR VOTE YOU IN...**

36

99. SHARE THE DOUGH

(Tune: "Let it Snow")
(New words: Julie McCall)

WHILE THE MINIMUM WAGE IS FRIGHTFUL
FOR THE WEALTHY LIFE'S DELIGHTFUL
TELL THOSE MILLIONAIRE CEO'S
SHARE THE DOUGH, SHARE THE DOUGH,
     SHARE THE DOUGH!

THE BATTLE AROUND US RAGES
AS WE FIGHT FOR LIVING WAGES
AND WE WANT TO GET WHAT WE'RE OWED
SHARE THE DOUGH, SHARE THE DOUGH,
     SHARE THE DOUGH!

Chorus
WE LEAVE FAMILIES HOME AT NIGHT
WORKING TWO JOBS IS THE NORM
AND WE KNOW THAT IT'S JUST NOT RIGHT
THIS SYSTEM NEEDS SOME REFORM.

THE ECONOMY'S GLOBALIZING
IN THE STREETS WE'RE ORGANIZING
AND WE'RE MAKING OUR MOVEMENT GROW
SHARE THE DOUGH, SHARE THE DOUGH,
     SHARE THE DOUGH!!!

100. **SOLIDARITY FOREVER**

Tune: **Battle Hymn of the Republic**
Words: Ralph Chaplin

WHEN THE UNION'S INSPIRATION
THRU THE WORKER'S BLOOD SHALL RUN
THERE CAN BE NO POWER GREATER
ANYWHERE BENEATH THE SUN
FOR WHAT FORCE ON EARTH IS WEAKER
THAN THE FEEBLE STRENGTH OF ONE
FOR THE UNION MAKES US STRONG.

Chorus:

SOLIDARITY FOREVER (3X)
FOR THE UNION MAKES US STRONG.

THEY HAVE TAKEN UNTOLD MILLIONS
THAT THEY NEVER TOILED TO EARN
BUT WITHOUT OUR BRAIN AND MUSCLE
NOT A SINGLE WHEEL CAN TURN
WE CAN BREAK THEIR HAUGHTY POWER
GAIN OUR FREEDOM WHEN WE LEARN
THAT THE UNION MAKES US STRONG.

IN OUR HANDS IS PLACED A POWER
GREATER THAN THEIR HOARDED GOLD
GREATER THAN THE MIGHT OF ARMIES
MAGNIFIED A THOUSAND- FOLD
WE CAN BRING TO BIRTH A NEW WORLD
FROM THE ASHES OF THE OLD
FOR THE UNION MAKES US STRONG

Chorus in Spanish:

SOLIDARIDAD POR SIEMPRE

SOLIDARIDAD POR SIEMPRE

SOLIDARIDAD POR SIEMPRE

QUE VIVA LA UNION

(or CON LA FUERZA

Spanish verse: **SINDICAL)**

LLEVEREMOS EN LA SANGRE

LA GRANDEZA SINDICAL

NO TENDRA PODER MAS GRANDE

EL LABORISMO MUNDIAL

COMPANERO SI ERES DEBIL

CON TU FUERZA INDIVIDUAL

QUE VIVA LA UNION.

ROCKIN' SOLIDARITY FOREVER (CHORUS)

(It's great when you jazz it up with a chorus like this:)

COME ON PEOPLE, NOW - SOLIDARITY FOREVER

EVERYBODY NEEDS - SOLIDARITY FOREVER

PEOPLE CRYING FOR - SOLIDARITY FOREVER

IT'S THE UNION-YEAH THE UNION MAKES US

THE UNION - YEAH- THE UNION MAKES US

THE UNION - YEAH- THE UNION MAKES US STRONG!

A FEW ADDITIONAL WORDS...

IN THESE TIMES OF RENEWED ACTIVISM AND ORGANIZING, GOOD CHANTS AND SONGS CAN BE IMPORTANT ORGANIZING AND ENERGIZING TOOLS AND CAN REALLY BRIGHTEN A PICKETLINE AND RALLY.

A PICKETLINE IS IN ITS GLORY WHEN IT HAS A FEW LOUD NOISEMAKERS TO KEEP THE STEP LIVELY AND THE SPIRIT STRONG!!! HOMEMADE NOISEMAKERS WORK GREAT AND ARE SO EASY TO MAKE. SHAKERS USING EMPTY SODA CANS AND FILLED WITH BEANS, PEBBLES OR BALLBEARINGS AND COVERED WITH TAPE CAN MAKE A POWERFUL SOUND. WHISTLES, BICYCLE HORNS, COWBELLS AND DRUMS MADE OF POTS, PANS AND SPOONS SOUND GREAT, TOO.

SINGING ON A PICKETLINE REALLY MOVES THINGS ALONG. MANY POPULAR SONGS -ROCK, COUNTRY, FOLK, REGGAE AND HOLIDAY - CAN BE GIVEN CLEVER AND POWERFUL NEW WORDS. SOME WONDERFUL EXAMPLES ARE INCLUDED INSIDE.

The RAGING GRANNIES songs are terrific!
Check them out on line.

GOODCHANTS FOR A LIVELY PICKETLINE IS INTENDED AS A READY RESOURCE FOR ANY ACTION. THESE 'ZIPPER' CHANTS AND SONGS ARE EASILY ADAPTED TO ANY SITUATION- JUST 'ZIP IN' YOUR GROUP, YOUR ISSUES AND YOU'RE GOOD TO GO! PASS IT AROUND, SHARE IT AND ABOVE ALL- USE IT TO BUILD A BETTER WORLD. WE HOPE THIS LITTLE BOOK HELPS!

Ruth Goldbaum©2002

41

34

44

52

53